UNEXPRESSED
Feelings

UNEXPRESSED FEELINGS
Copyright © 2016 Khadija Rupa.

http://khadijarupa.tumblr.com/

Editor: Hend Hegazi
Book Design: Niyah Press

Cover Artist: Liza's Brushes

ISBN: 978-1-945873-00-3

ATTENTION: SCHOOLS AND BUSINESSES
Khadija Rupa books are available at quantity discounts with bulk purchase for educational, business, or sales promotional use. For information, please visit the author at:
http://khadijarupa.tumblr.com/

UNEXPRESSED
Feelings

Written By
KHADIJA RUPA

About the Book:

Unexpressed Feelings is a book which begins with the unbearable melancholy that creeps under one's skin, into the bones, when an unexpected heartbreak takes place. Priceless lessons, that only mistakes and sorrow can teach, leap out from the middle part of the book with the forethought to heal an inner wound that is still raw, still painful. This book of yearning, heartache and realisations gradually comes to a beautiful end in part three by unveiling how love is supposed to look like when it truly enters one's life. By expressing some of the sweet feelings of falling in love and being consumed by it in this last section, with the right person this time, the aim of the book is one: to give hope to souls that propels them to the continuous search for *Love. True Love.*

Throughout this book, loss, lessons and love have been portrayed in a brief, whimsical, poetic manner with meanings that are intensely deep.

About the Author:

With writings consisting of genuine feelings rather than mere words, Khadija Rupa, a contemporary author, has already attracted a worldwide following of many wonderful souls. Her uncanny ability to express complex feelings with simplicity has made her well known for fixing broken hearts.

Many of her readers affirm that through her writings they find instant relief since some of her personal beliefs serve as life-changing reminders for them. Currently she is writing the sequel to this book, exploring deep emotions with the hope to unveil more unexpressed aches, more epiphanies.

More longings.

For Sumel—

Even before we met,
    I've known you in a way.

As if since the beginning of existence,
    we two have been soul mates.

Special Thanks—

When everyone's eyes
have been designed
to see what is visible,

she, my mother,
breaks all the rules
and sees the soul.

Contents

Part One:
Crying Is Allowed Here 1

Part Two:
School of Lost Souls   87

Part Three:
Darling It's Me: Love!   133

Part One

Crying Is Allowed Here

Soul's Void

Do you love me enough
       that I am allowed
       to be damaged?

Do you love me enough
       that I am allowed
       to be weak in some places?

That I am allowed
       to not be
       the fairytale?

That when I am so hungry,
       you would feed me so much love
       that I can't take it any more?

The Change

You promised me once,
> the emotions we blossomed together,
> nothing would ever wither,
> not even in the darkest of nights.

Then came the days,
> day after day,
> month after month,
> year after year,

that it's nothing and no one else,
> but your own protected-love,
> that un-protected me,
> even in the brightest of daylights.

....

Do you know why you keep saying that things are not going to work between us the way they used to before? She was overly irritated this time.

We can always go back to the time when everything was like a dream between us. But the problem is, she looks at him angrily, *you will go there to meet me. And you are not the you I used to know back then.*

Inequality

When you hurt me,
      I hurt you, too.

The only difference is:
      I hurt you
      just for a little time,
      right at the moment
      when you hurt me,
      with an unexpected wound
      lasting a lifetime.

An Unfair Loss

You owned me
    in a way,
    I never wanted
    to be owned.

I owned you
    in a way,
    you never thought
    someone ever would.

To you I gave,
    what you wanted to have;
    to me you gave,
    what you wanted to get;

In all my giving
    love for you was pure;
    in all your getting
    loss was just mine, for sure.

Complicated We

The words of your hands,
          the promises of your touch,
          the whispers of your silence,
          are all a language,
          I don't understand.

The hands of my words,
          the touch of my promises,
          the silence of my whispers,
          are all a language,
          you don't understand.

Unpromising

Your promises
        are like a dark night.

Without any moon,
        without any stars.

In them,
        I see no light.

Blank History

Yesterday
  you were
  my I.

But today
  you are
  my you.

Gradually taking both of us
    towards a tomorrow
    with no I, no you.

When You Hurt

I know exactly where it aches
        when I am hurt
        by the people for whom I care.

But when it's you,
        it doesn't hurt me
        just anywhere,
        not here or there.

I feel the pain—
        everywhere.

The Saddest Thing

She pretends,
        she doesn't.

He pretends,
        he doesn't, too.

And they can't understand,
        what hurts more—

Missing the other person,
        or pretending not to.

Crying in the Shower

When the people,
      who wake you up
         from—dreams,

start waking you up,
      so horrifically,
         from—nightmares.

False Empathy

When I tried to tell you
        so many things,
        you claimed—
        you knew everything.

Today when there is nothing
        left to say,
        in your silence I realise,
        you knew nothing.

        Not a single thing.

Mean

The people who mean the most,
  in the end, always become
  the ones who are mean—the most.

It's not an overreaction.
  It's not a matter of who is weak
  and who is strong.

I find it hard and indigestible,
  that the moment you let somebody go,
  they walk off and never look back.

Why don't they try?
  And if they do why do they not
  persist until convincing you?

Someone is always there.
  Even here. But only when—
  I hold on to them.

Self Torture

In all my haste,
        I attached myself
        to an unfeeling soul,
        to whom neither I belong,
        nor must I ever own.

The backbone of my voice fractures
        as I invent words,
        using all the metaphors
        using all the aches,
        I ever came to know.

My tears blur my vision,
        watching you move on
        so very quickly,
        whilst I still,
        don't want to let go.

The Unexpressed Ache

I do want—
>to walk away,
>to release you,
>and let both of us live.

But I can't—
>I know if I do,
>you won't ever
>come after me.

That's what—
>hurts the most.
>That's what,
>breaks me the most.

....

Would you miss me ever again?

I don't know. He says. *Maybe. Or maybe not. There's no difference between the two anymore, right?* He asks. Or maybe he answers.

Heartbreaker

All her life she believed—
      a Princess
      she could be.

But deep down,
      somewhere far within,
      she knew he would never
      conduct himself—
      like a charming Prince.

One Way Love

A thousand hopes
           in a hundred dreams,
           under my skies
           fly all your whims.

The heavy screams
           my heart squeals,
           why only to me
           are they distinct?

The hope we sew
           hung on a finish line,
           the love I gave you
           all its pain is only mine.

A Black Lie

Things you saw
      in my eyes,
      were the only things
      you ever desired.

Yet when I was hurt,
      you so easily blamed,
      said I never heeded—
      all the things you cared.

Misunderstanding

I thought,
> you came
> from a world—

Where I enter
> to dream.

It's Over

He cried that day.
　　All day,
　　all night.

She cried, too.
　　Sadly,
　　all her life.

Closure

Nothing has been
sorted out—

I reminded the universe again and again
        with loudness
        that was deadly silent.

Yet our book
        was being closed;
        the mystery remained unsolved.

We were folded, and stamped—
        as the unfinished story
        in a forgotten history.

When There's Nothing Left to Say

Beyond all our times of ending
        until it came to an unconditional end,
        I will meet you in such a way
        that you will wake up
        and call it—a dream.

I will speak to you
        in a way unspoken,
        neither you will hear
        nor will it be ever clear,
        yet you will call it—silence.

A destination we left far behind,
        I will remind you of its triumph
        in such a way,
        you will keep moving on
        and call it—forgotten.

Moving On

It's you,
>> whom I always
>> wanted to keep.

But now the feelings,
>> once I had for you,
>> are completely gone.

It's a poem,
>> of our love,
>> that doesn't rhyme.

A story,
>> never meant to have,
>> a happy end.

Broken Dreams

My tears risked their lives
　　　　climbing down a precipitous cliff
　　　　of dreams in total darkness and grief;

I could clearly see
　　　　how tightly every drop
　　　　held a piece of me.

Please don't tell me,
　　　　it was less painful
　　　　than a broken backbone,
　　　　a forgotten poem,
　　　　a lost home.

....

They tell me, that my eyes are intense, and speak louder.

"What do you see through them?" they ask me.
"Stories I couldn't live," my hands reply.

Loving Him

Swimming to the impossible shore
    when my ship wrecked
    amidst the ocean—
    felt like loving him.

Throwing away my unpublished manuscript,
    that took years and years
    to complete—
    felt like loving him.

Shrinking and suffocating in a corner,
    when everyone else
    celebrated my victory—
    felt like loving him.

When We Two Parted

The sun still left on time,
        time didn't stop either;
        the ocean was still silent,
        the sky was still there.

I thought,
        today the sun would be late for others,
        time would stumble;
        the ocean would rage in war,
        the sky would definitely fall over.

But my world fell apart,
        and all they could do,
        the whole universe,
        was to silently move on.

I am Nowhere

Whenever my own time becomes
        a stranger;
        whenever my own breeze becomes
        a stranger;
        my own silence becomes
        a stranger;
        my own solitary becomes
        a stranger;

when to recognise the voice
        I have been hearing
        since the beginning,
        I struggle;
        when to understand the words
        I have been speaking
        since the first day,
        I wrangle,

my heart stops beating.
        It blinks.
        My eyes stop blinking.
        They beat.
        With the same pause.
        With the same hope.
        That someday,
        even my existence would be felt.

I Don't Want to Know

I still don't know exactly why you left,
      and why you forgot
      long before you should.

Why you decided not to try,
      and why you didn't stop
      seeing me cry.

Why you didn't look back
      and why later
      you came back.

And then why,
      once again, you left,
      without saying farewell.

I just know, some answers
      shouldn't have
      questions;

And some questions,
      mustn't have
      any answers.

Well Wishes

When you are tired
    of avoiding and detaching;

when you are tired
    of coming and going;

when you are tired
    of running and running;

    look back.

Where you left me—
    you will find my dreams standing.

Restart the life,
    with them have your new beginnings.

How?

It wasn't,
>a story,
>I wanted for my life.

The girl whose
>favourite characters
>are always—
>*the kind ones,*

the girl whose
>every novel
>ends with—
>*happily ever after,*

the girl whose
>book covers are always—
>*the world of fairy tales,*

how could
>she be
>someone's mistake?

A Rootless Wanderer

My eyes, my two eyes wide open; with their blurred vision, their wetness, their unheard voice, I touch the entire sky. The feeling I get when they move together to the right, the difference I see in the left part of the dawn sky—I wonder, if the colours are entering into my dark eyes, or if I am the one who is sending all my colours to the whole dark world outside.

I touch the mountains, of the earth, of the ocean. I touch their rigidness, their waiting, their calling; my eyes wide open, in awe. In prostration I hold the entire universe's weight not on my knees, not on my toes, not on my forehead but on my two squeezed eyelids.

My hands never touched the words that crushed a whole heart of mine in between. My ten fingers, all calm; my palms, fearlessly straight, but my eyes touched it all. They touched the salty-pain, the heart-floor, too, the time I was a new-born. They touched, and touched and touched and when my eyes gradually close, I wonder, if I pull the entire world's darkness into them, or if I give away to the world—all my light.

....

Your smile is unbelievably beautiful, he muttered somberly into her ears. *I can feel how terribly you keep falling apart behind it.*

A Hope That
Hurts Most

Love is a separation
        where two people believe,
        they would be together
        once again where
        end meets forever.

Love is waiting,
        till the last breath.

And sometimes,
        even after that.

Happiness

Every time I am told
       something is going to come true
       the way I wished it,
       I wait holding the whole universe
       within me.

The moment arrives,
       strangely everything
       gets postponed
       and I wait again,
       never losing hope.

Until later I hear,
       we are sorry,
       your happiness—
       has been cancelled.

Generous Grief

Every single thing,
      every single person
      gives so little,
      even when I request more;

      please some more.

When the turn comes,
      for grief to give,
      it overflows
      my life's shore.

The Universe Through my Window

(The Second Type of Loneliness)

I wake up in the middle of night and my own bedroom feels unknown. As if I am somewhere extremely far—like on the end of the Solar System where there is no gravity and I can see this immense planet slowly rotating on its orbit without any support right in front of me. I am so close to it that I can even hear the creepy sound of its rotation…and it's almost deafening me.

And there are moons, so many scary, massive moons. Like five hundred moons. Some stars are so different from what they look like from my planet; they seem so horrible that if I touched them I would instantly burn to ashes. And some are like a black spider's infinite white toes—just as tiny as I used to see from Earth. But from here, everything feels more real. So real that I tremble. I suffocate. I have no air to breathe yet desperately convince my heart to keep beating. And I scream, hoping someone from Earth will hear me and wake everyone else saying—*Guys! I heard a cry, someone needs us terribly.*

But I am so far. My legs already heavy blocks of concrete. The thoughts of never being heard, that no one will ever come to know where I am or what I am doing, that even if

I try, I can't go back to my own beautiful planet—make me lose my balance and I fall. And I am rolling, I'm still rolling. I want to stop myself, hold myself tight with my two hands but then I realise even there is a place within human hearts where forces like gravity—don't work. I just keep rolling. Keep falling.

A Meaningless Expectation

The sun has disappeared
        behind a summer cloud.

Now only a heavy mass,
        of thick water vapour,
        floating all around.

A worry,
        an anger,
        a sorrow,
        pouring down all over.

I know I expected too much,
        I am sorry for being such;
        as I mistook thinking,
        for you I would do as much.

A Prayer That Came True

I always prayed,
       with courage and confidence,
       no matter how unbearable it seemed,
       that I may ease your grief
       by having it filled up in me.

Maybe this is why so unexpectedly,
       a small tap
       broke our unbreakable bond;
       and for a lifetime I became,
       an incurable wound.

Stranger

I told you
> a thousand beautiful words.
> You understood all of them.

I told you
> A silence.
> You remained silent.

I told you
> a thousand tears.
> Now you are a stranger.

My Wasted Sacrifice

I liked you,
      for what you weren't.
      You disliked me,
      for what I wasn't.

Your life is,
      as it was,
      without me.

My life is,
      as it was,
      when you killed me.

But I'm used to all these pains;
      from the beginning I knew—
      between two forevers,
      only the worst can be true.

Emptiness

I knew who I was
        before you appeared;
        I admit life wasn't filled to the brim,
        but at least it wasn't fully empty.

When you came,
        you were always near,
        you were everywhere,
        until you were here, there, nowhere.

Now the harder I try,
        the more I struggle,
        who was I—
        before we met?

Sshhhh!

The eerie movement
      of the three hands
      of my ghostly wall clock.

Its tick-tock, tick-tock, tick-tock,
      from four a.m.
      to four p.m.

Reminds me nothing
      but how quiet and how slow
      suddenly my whole world became.

Remembering You In My Forgetfulness

Once I asked you, *will you ever forget me?* You replied just like every crazy lover does—"I *couldn't* even if I wanted to."

Now, many times I sit at my window, in my beautiful autumn bed, and still keep missing home. The pages that are torn from my poetry books, I can't tell what I have actually done to them. And even photographs pinned on my walls started to appear unfamiliar a long time ago. When some unknown people, who still claim to be my old friends, heard some sad news related to me, they beat me, tried to get me to cry just for once. I tried earnestly to expand my little soul to fill the whole universe just to force myself to laugh. Because now when I even forgot how to cry, I need helplessly to laugh. That's the only way left to squeeze out my tears. That's the only way now I cry.

I don't even know exactly how long it has been since we started living in two different parts of the same world. Wasn't it all two years ago? Is there a zero, too, after two? But why do I feel there are two, three, four and five zeros?

Again, I don't know.

Today, however, I feel proud of myself. That someday I replied to the same question I questioned you: That, "even if I *can*, even if I forget everything, myself, too—never will I—you."

Treacherous Market Of Love

Like a single raindrop
        melting into a river
        that flows into the ocean,
        what was once visible
        only to my eyes,
        gradually all of it disappeared.

Clouds of white ache,
        in the far corner of a sky
        that only birds of dusk own,
        covered all that once
        I thought I would own.

If ever again,
        someone says
        to go to the market,
        where hearts are sold
        in exchange for melancholy souls,
        never would I go.

Never would I wait,
        if ever again
        someone says—
        not to.

Winter Cries

I have entered an unknown
    no grey can ever reach.
    I have been in a cosmos
    no emptiness can ever know.

I have breathed a melancholy
    no ear can ever hear.
    I have a day which secretes dark
    no night can ever bear.

I have a story curled up in my bed
    no one can ever fall asleep with.
    I have a red
    no winter can ever bleed.

A Melancholy Soul

She has the clearest road;
  a magical lamppost,
  to guide her soul that's lost
  somewhere deep within.

She says,
  the road will take her nowhere,
  or perhaps
  somewhere back to nowhere?

Grey clouds
  are always better
  to sit under,
  she whispers.

Black Sun

For a long time
       I haven't seen
       the sun.

All around me
       even the bright days
       look so dark.

Among all the complex knots
       of yours I had undone,
       it's your disgracing words
       still left undone.

Among all the cries
       that make me feel better,
       I'm still trying to be fine.

Shackles Of Iron

Sky's piercing gaze
        grasps me for a moment;
        my legs sinking down
        to my own bottomless base.

My dark seems to swirl,
        around and around,
        changing from the color of night
        to a dawn of blue sound.

To my surprise
        an unseen ache clutches me,
        holds me suspended in the air,
        commanding all my grounds to disappear.

Disappearance Of Time

Thousand decades have passed
      within this one quiver,
      with all the different seasons
      only as winter.

A small piece of sleep,
      a small piece of blur,
      fiercely dipped
      in the eyes of water.

Malaise

It is to keep walking
        not because you want to
        but because you have to;

that the long grueling day ends,
        she looks at the mirror
        by mistake,
        and with such a pang, murmurs—

I don't know
        this girl.

Neither do I
        want to.

Sadly Ever After

Once upon a time, there was a little princess who was deeply in love with sad poems, sad words, and sad endings. She was the sad princess. While all her friends were busy enjoying happy endings of fairy tales, she used to write heart-rending poetry in her secret diary. All the sorrowful moments of her life and the lives of her loved ones, all the lyrics of her tears and melodies of her cries, used to built a safe shelter in her secret diary's world. The moment something or someone upset her, she would find comfort by reading this diary.

When she grew up, one day her mother, the queen, fixed her marriage with the prince of a far away kingdom who had an extraordinary talent to make people grin. He was a happy prince. After all, the queen was desperate to see her daughter smiling. On the wedding night, when the sad princess saw the happy prince smiling at her, she was mesmerised. She had never seen a smile like his in her entire life. It instantly sent light to her dark blue world and lifted up all her darkness to the sky. She understood the feeling of being pleased is a million times different than that of being gloomy. Sadness makes one fearless of losing something, but happiness scares. And she was ready to be scared of losing this happy prince so she started spending all her seconds, minutes and hours, smiling and laughing with him.

After a couple of years the prince realised it had been a very long time since he had gone outside. So the next morning he went out in the forest to hunt. For the first time the princess felt his absence. It was terrible; so much so that it reminded her of sadness and she immediately took her forgotten diary and started reading it.

When the prince returned from hunting in the evening, he unexpectedly saw her crying while reading the diary. He was amazed; the sound of her crying was wonderfully melodious. And the way her tears rolled down from her eyes to her lap seemed like the lyrics of a sweet poem soaked with souls. He grasped her chin with both his hands as the red ache he saw all over her face blew him away. Her dense green eyes, her wet plump cheeks, the curved corner of her small lips—everything was perfectly filled with a gorgeous grief. Every time her tearful eyelids moved up and down, he kept falling for her again and again. *How can a sorrowful face be so beautiful and innocent?* he asked himself, stunned. As if happiness makes one fearless of losing something, but sadness scares.

And the prince was desperate to be scared of losing the princess so from that day, he never made her smile again. He only gave her gifts of sad poems, sad words and sad endings. He bought thousands of melancholy books and gave her all. In return, all he wanted was to see her sad; crying all the time, being his sadly ever after.

....

Do you love me? she asks.
Even if you don't love me in return, my love for you will be enough for both of us.

Sad Girls

She made a severe mistake,
  by hearing all the silence
  that he never did speak.

She made a mistake again,
  by wanting him from a distance
  he never promised to shorten.

The mistake,
  that was worst of all,
  she hid some feelings
  that made her fall
  for him even more.

Now when she expresses
  her longing,
  she ends up losing him
  more than ever before.

Secret Sorrows

You were yours,
      I was yours.

What was yours,
      was solely yours.

What was mine,
      was all yours, too.

What was ours,
      is now all untrue.

Strange You

You said once,
        my flaws mean nothing to you
        as long as I believe they are flaws.

You said,
        what is ours
        is what comes from each of us.

You said again,
        I'm the one
        who would always be your last.

You said,
        our love would grow
        a little more every day
        and would be a little too much.

And then you didn't say,
        on a stormy night
        you just disappeared.

Unexpressed Feelings

Today her morning slid very slowly, quietly, surreptitiously under her misery. Today she cried. Cried and cried, opening every door within her and lifting up all the veils from all those excruciating memories that secretly torture her. Today she lay in bed with all her wounds bare and open.

The morning was so slow in its movement that she felt every individual drop of blood slithering under her skin, heart, and mind. Every drop falling on the floor, on the pillow from her soul, she could clearly hear their echoes. When it became night's turn to wring her, morning was still unfinished. Terrified morning sought shelter under her tiring eyelids, shining and burning her up inside so fiercely with its darkness that even the sleep suffocated and left her helplessly.

"Are you okay?" No one ever asked her.

"Go away!!!" she screamed, falling violently to her knees, suddenly dumb, shocked by her own reaction.

Flashbacks

You loved me,
        so much just yesterday;
        today you don't even
        want to stay.

Once I had,
        a minor finger-cut,
        you were the one
        to bleed so hard.

Now you pass by
        and pretend,
        as if on Earth,
        not a single injustice happened.

But I'll pretend, too,
        it comforts me,
        hoping someday—
        it actually will.

....

What about those Promises of yours to never leave me? she asked, stammering too much this time. His cruel smirk was as gut-wrenching as his words—*Promises are meant to be broken, sweetheart.*

Her Nights

"Was it a nightmare again?" he asked, terrified.

"No," she fought to keep her expression as normal as possible. However his watchful eyes stayed fixed on hers. "I saw you were crying in your sleep," he continued when she would not reply. "Whom were you trying to bring back today?"

Her face became as black as the moonless night sky. "I was asking the same question to the same people," her voice dropped a little lower.

"And you were trying to convince them to come back, to love you just a little bit, but, as usual, they left you overlooked…" he murmured, eyes and hands too tight.

Special Power (Part One)

In life sometimes, unintentionally, we commit a ghastly mistake which makes us feel so remorseful that in a flash, this one mistake reminds us of all the mistakes we ever committed in our entire lives, but never noticed. Or maybe we were arrogant enough to accept.

In a dark place, deep down in the very ground we stand on, we find ourselves held captive, suffocating, pressing our backbone hard against the wall and sinking our head between two trembling arms, as if nothing in this world matters except those mistakes.

This is a painfully special moment as a special power enters us, piercing every cell of the body like bullets of world war fifty three. We start to notice the tears of the people whom we've hurt on our hands and clothes as if blood suddenly decided to change its colour to that of water. And the ache they went through because of us brings us to our knees, paralyzes us from even breathing. Then it owns this outstanding quality to teach us all those valuable lessons that maybe, maybe we wouldn't have learnt at any other time, in any other way— transforming us to a person—who is ready and prepared to pay any cost to amend all those mistakes.

I want this special power to enter your body, too. There is a place where a secret part of empty-handed and crestfallen people go to seek this power. They wear black shawls and a thick cloud of tiny water droplets suspended in the atmosphere. I want you to find that dreadful place and hear their terrifying cries. And then to search for me there impatiently, screaming my name again and again, pulling out every nerve wrapped around your throat with your two trembling hands. The way I did once. But I hope you don't feel the hurt as much as I did.

You are too weak and fragile to stand that ache. Remember, *you always will be.*

Special Power (Part Two)

"Why do you think some people wish the person whom they had once loved unconditionally to realise someday how much they had hurt them? Do you think it's because they want this person to suffer or to come back?" He asked her while washing his black shiny Volvo car.

"Of course neither," she said, tying a piece of cloth around the injured leg of the parrot she had found in the garden. "Someone who knows how to love unconditionally and was hurt by an extreme pain would never want anyone else to experience such intense pain, let alone a beloved."

"Then why do they say—*one day, you will realise*?" He asked as he continued wiping the window glass, without looking at her.

"See, there are two kinds of realisations: one that leaves you in suffering so that you get destroyed and another that leaves you in suffering so that you get built. That's what they want: to see their beloved get built."

"Get built?" His moist forehead wrinkled, the confusion preventing him from closing the car door, and he just turned around and stared at her.

She threw the bird up to the bright sky and watched with joy as it flew away. "You see," she took a deep breath, "the one who hurts someone in a way that wrecks their soul beyond repair, can heal many impossible wounds of the world if he realises his cruel mistake. They transform themselves to a special power. The bravery, the strength they build in themselves to heal others by hurting someone else, one can hardly build it by being hurt by someone else." She continued looking at the empty sky while joy played tug of war against a mystery in her face.

He approached her and started helping her to clean her hands from the stains of blood. His chest had been aching agonizingly since the morning remembering the way she had cried secretly last night. "Doesn't that mean," honey started to melt in his quiet tone, "it is because of the people who love unconditionally that such miraculous healers get built? As one mostly realises their mistake in such a life-changing way when they accept that they wrecked someone who has loved them unconditionally. Doesn't that mean," his tone incredibly calm with both eyes fighting to escape her own, "it is the unbearable wound of people who love unconditionally that heals the incurable wound of the world? Doesn't that mean, the world is helplessly in need of their ache, too?"

She stared at him in shock. She instantly understood, some questions are asked not to question, but those questions themselves are eye-opening answers.

I Wonder

Do you ever wonder
> where the nightingale disappears
> on nights that are longer and darker?

Do you ever wonder
> if I ever truly slept after you left me
> with a pain that was eternally sleepless?

Do you ever wonder
> if your decision was as right for you
> as it slowly started to be for me?

Do you ever wonder, do you,
> why I loved you for such a long time,
> and still didn't really know you?

Thunderstorm

Now even if she smiles,
        it seems a lost girl
        is crying.

And don't ask me
        how it sounds
        when she laughs
        her heart out.

Deafening thunders
        in a thunderstorm
        are always
        less frightful.

If

They ask me forever,
>>how I stay with cracks and splits,
>>all over my body,
>>ghastly un-repaired.

How I walk around
>>with wounds that are raw,
>>and intolerably putrid,
>>to the heart and soul.

What things would I give
>>to stitch my torn skin;
>>through what situation would I live
>>to make it glowingly new within?

I tell them forever,
>>I would give the whole world.
>>Without a single shiver,
>>I would live through it all.

But if ever I try to mend,
>>some other bodies
>>would instantly break,
>>would instantly be fragments.

The Difference

I gave you such happiness,
> which once recalled,
> would replace—
> even the greatest sorrow of yours.

You gave me such sorrow,
> which in a lifetime impossible to forget;
> even the greatest of happiness—
> cannot ever replace those.

Law Of Conversion

Like poetry, physics has always been a mystery to me. Both are my favourite, too. Everything about these two subjects always teaches me something fascinating and eternal about the universe. And about us...about you and me. Hence, despite all that's happened, I continue to believe—*our love was never unreal.*

It even follows, *the law of conversion*. This law states that energy can neither be created nor destroyed, but can always change its form. I find it the perfect definition of our love. Do you remember how we used to say—if you truly love someone, then there won't be anything which can affect the quantity and quality of your love? Not even the sun or moon can do that using time as their weapon. Love can't be created, neither increased nor decreased. It's as it was at the beginning and will always be the same throughout, till the ending. That's the science of love: it is always at its peak. And so when we fell in love with each other, we instantly knew we could never love each other more than—*this.*

And love can't be destroyed; at least that's what we used to promise each other, remember? Truly, we didn't lie.

In our lives, love, like energy, has just changed its form. Yours has changed into an unsaid goodbye, an unfelt emotion. And by reminding myself every morning that you don't exist anymore in my world, my love keeps changing itself into many different forms. Sometimes it becomes the night of the desert, sometimes the day of the ocean, and sometimes an ache—which is meant to appear just before the *historic healing*, just before the *tremendous transformation*.

Just before the *majestic moment* where I find myself by losing everything.

A Lovesickness

I hope someday the sun will still rise from the same east it has been rising since the beginning. I hope, that day, even the cloudless sky will remain as blue as it should be naturally. Those gray sparrows playing outside my closed-window, I hope none of them die. The hands, of trees dressed full in colours, keep unclothing season after season. The busy streets bustling with human sounds never become empty.

Nothing ever changes, not even my favourite library, not even my favourite lake, not even me, only you. I hope someday you change when nothing changes: neither in the universe nor in me. And surprise me as you say: *I understand.*

And I will wear the same old gown you made from red and gave me when you proposed. And I will wear the same white pearls that you tied on my right ankle when I accepted your soul. Then I will hold both your hands; you will clearly hear my spirit laughing. Slowly I will take you to everywhere we ever were just to show what it looks like when time stops. Life stops. Living stops. Until then I will live to prevent as many changes as I can. Until then, I hope to understand.

Never Again

Never again, will I say anything.

The emptiness deep within
        has started
        to deepen again.

My soul is being wounded more,
        from my tattered feelings
        to my battered thoughts.

But never again, will I show any of that.

What has gone,
        what was never near,
        how I ache to be there.

But never again, will I ever look back.
        Never again,
        will I say anything.

When Hands Unhold

An undiscovered prayer at the end of the galaxy
    falling through space like a meteor;
    amidst all the worlds pulled by gravity,
    I have surely lost you somewhere.

From all my dreams where you felt everlasting
    to all my clothes your words used to wear,
    to the old end, to the new beginning,
    you have lost me everywhere.

A Cruel Reminder

Sometimes some forgotten memories,
        on a delightfully decorated day,
        knock my mended-heart to congratulate—
        I have successfully forgotten those
        moments,
        when so badly my heart was broken.

Thus, I fail to forget—
        those unforgettable memories,
        those unforgettable aches,
        which many a time I keep forgetting,
        and I only want to forget.

Poet's Last Line

Why do you want a sad poet to be one of your soul mates?

"I want to be the last line of his poetry," she replies. "There's a truth, an eternity, a breathtaking sadness hidden behind those last words. And between a poet and his heart, all around him, his left, his right—a musical silence sings just like the blue of the sky, like the white of the moon, like all the twinkles that fall from the stars' soundless tunes. In that silence, I dream to be."

Do you think you will ever find one?

When something is very complicated, or very uncomplicated, it becomes harder to explain. Maybe this is why she doesn't want to answer this question. Her wet eyes slowly squint, themselves searching for a thousand answers, for a thousand explanations. And when she finally decides to reply, she says, she always says—

"This is why I write."

Illogical Truth

That *moment* when you are writing a story and suddenly you stand up, run to a quite place where you would be completely unnoticed and cry your heart out.

After some time, you come back to the table—where the non-dairy creamer is now floating on the surface of your freezing coffee, some anguished adjectives stand out from a few crumpled pages, as though they're sticking their tongues out at you, a few fountain pens mock your emptiness with their own and an old wall clock is your only sympathizer, pretending that time has stopped—now you can quit—and suddenly you change your mind and decide not to finish the story. Or maybe you'll do it some other time, when you are whole enough. Or broken enough. In either case, no one reaches an unbreakable state.

A Question

"How do you know when it's over?" the world asks him.

"When you look at her and instantly know this is a girl whom men have been losing since the beginning of time. This is a girl for whom many mortals became immortal. This is a girl for which poetry ends up giving birth to poets. This is a girl you can't keep.

You aren't allowed to."

The Heartless Girl

I was quite surprised to see you standing on a doorstep that, as far as I believed, was mine. Unexpected things had stopped appearing there a long time ago.

It was painfully beautiful yet beautifully strange to know it was you who had found my purse under the oak tree of that lake. I couldn't imagine someone like you would go there. I thought only people who keep running from their own selves rush there every weekend taking a taxi that takes approximately six hours and fifteen minutes to reach. There they tear their chest apart, pull out their heart, their lungs, their ribcage and throw them into the small lake. Entirely empty, they breathe freedom sitting under the oak tree as long as the day allows. When dusk comes down, they search the whole lake, realising they aren't allowed to stay empty for long. They have to go back where they don't want to go. They put their heart, lungs, and ribcage back and stitch their chest with a thread of blue ache.

I didn't even notice that evening I left my purse there. You called my best friend and I realised why my cell phone had been merciful toward me all night. Although I requested her to collect it from you, she is always up to something that might give my life—*a beginning*.

You drove six hours to reach me and when I saw you for the first time at the bottom of those stairs—white T-shirt, grey unzipped cardigan, grey Nike trainers, short stubble, brown eyes, summer smile—I was actually trying to remember where I had seen you before. The way your curious eyes were chasing mine when I stood in front of you, I knew I had known these eyes before. You said you unintentionally read some of my poetry from my phone while searching for a contact to reach me, and from there you felt a strong urge to meet me. I became compelled to question you with a stare that never takes any help from words. You heard me. Clearly. Loudly. You answered, the world suddenly started to feel like the wrong place. There are a lot of things we don't understand and what is worse is we don't understand that we don't understand.

The way you expressed yourself to a stranger like me, assured me it was you whom I had met in that small dark bookstore at the end of my small town. You were sitting somewhere on the fifth shelf of the last cupboard and I quietly cried out when I found you. Your tall height reminded me, that day I struggled to stand on my toes in order to hold you. Your dust painted my two hands with worlds beyond worlds that we are never allowed to see in any science books.

That day I brought you home and read you the whole night, page by page, word for word. Sometimes I sniffed your yellow and worn out parts. I threw myself so far in your depth that it took me a month to come out and notice I was actually sitting in my room. Nowhere else. Not with you.

I know I didn't even thank you. I just took my purse and closed the door in your face. I don't know if you stood there in shock, or left instantly. I don't know what you were thinking and if you wanted to meet me again or if you thought of stealing my poetry that would forever stay unpublished. But that's what I didn't want. I didn't want a story—*a beginning*. Not anymore. I have long ago stopped walking on a road where my dreams walk around. I change my destination a hundred times if I ever see an old wish of mine standing there in its real form. I don't know them. I don't want to. They too must not know me. They too must not recognise me as their owner.

Maybe you think I am a mean girl. I wish you could hear how I cried behind that same door, cuddling myself on the floor. That evening I read you again. All night. You were seeping through my skin and flowing into my veins. At four a.m. I clutched you to my chest and wept. The next day I didn't leave my bed. My curtains guarded me from the sun. And all day, I read you.

And all day—*I loved you.*

And wondered…

Maybe after fifty years, someday, somewhere, you will remember me and my poetry while telling stories to your grandchildren? I hope they learn and tell the next world, some people aren't meant to have a story in life, and that's absolutely okay as they become a story instead. Sometimes we finish all our right times meeting all the wrong people. This is why when the ones who are right—eventually appear—all we are left with is wrong times. Things could have been different between us. So, too, our stories.

If only we had met when I was ready to let the whole universe enter my heart.

Unreachable Soul

Where each season goes for celebration
       when not its turn
       to paint nature,
       you will find me there.

Where the cheerful children
       of unwritten poems,
       play all around,
       you will find me there.

Where the night sits
       beside the small window
       of a girl who collects moonlight
       in a black pitcher,
       you will always find me there.

Release

Where there is no law
of truth and lie,

where there is no rule
of wrong and right,

beyond what we wish, what we fear
and answered-prayers keep chasing
behind,

no obligations to explain,
no questions to ever answer;

only to close these eyes
to sleep in the lap of love
and stay there forever,

I will be found surely there,
even if the body is swallowed by earth—

only if ever
someone searches truly
and wants to find me.

Life Goes On (Part One)

Almasa. What should I tell you about her? She was a wonderful teenage girl who had the miraculous power to cure herself from any wound, either physical or mental. With her own salty tears, she would cleanse her raw wounds. And her breaths were given, as though not to breathe but, rather, to fan her sores.

The witty, six year old girl that used to play with her every afternoon, always teased her saying, "You are a blue sky that is completely hidden by the white cloud." When Sasma—that was how the little girl called Almasa—asked why, she always replied, "You look astonishingly stronger with teary eyes and heavy breaths but no one notices that. They think you are very weak." Hearing this, the smile that sometimes rippled in the corners of Almasa's otherwise frozen lips, was a melodious tune with no musical instruments.

One day, Almasa got injured again. This time her pain was so intense, she screamed as if a fire was burning her alive. All the people of her village including her own family urged her to let her tears stream down on the wound and to fan it with her breath so that it would heal, so she kept crying and breathing, breathing and crying. But the wound would not heal.

Time went by and that little girl Almasa used to play with, turned into a beautiful lady. In a beautiful twilight evening, a handsome knight married her and took her away to his castle far from the village. With time, she forgot Almasa.

After many years, this little girl turned into a cute old woman. Her face was glowing like a crumpled diamond. One afternoon she noticed the sky was completely cloudless, as if someone has just coloured it with pure blue paint. For the first time since her childhood, the memory of the beautiful self-healer knocked her aged mind. She remembered how the girl would heal her cuts and bruises with her own salty tears and seek all her peace by pouring her breaths into those deep sores. She hurried back to the village and asked for her. She did not even remember her name; all she remembered was how one day she was severely wounded and all the villagers advised her to keep crying and breathing.

"Almasa?" the farmer asked.

"Yes, yes Al...Almaasaa! Where is she? Is she fine? What happened to that wound? How did it heal? Did she..." The farmer replied even before she could finish, "Almasa is still there where she used to be."

"Her cave-like unlighted room," she abruptly whispered, knowing not how she recalled it.

Life Goes On (Part Two)

The minute she entered Almasa's room, she observed a very old woman, wrapped in wrinkled skin and wearing a grey dress matching her black and white twisted thread-like hair, sitting beside the broken window.

"Almasa!" she cried. But Almasa did not respond.

"Sasma?" This time she raised her shaky face in tiresomely slow motion and looked at her visitor. There was a minute of black in her fading eyes yet the smile she flashed later was as young as it used to be in those childhood days. It was only the music that was missing. And then without any words, any keenness, any curiosities, Almasa slowly lowered her shaky face again, and continued pouring her tears and puffing her breaths into the same wound that she'd been nursing for fifty years.

"Nothing has changed in her life except time? Can that ever happen in real life?" She wondered while leaving the room, deeply traumatized. A mass of grey cloud suddenly covered all the blue in the sky as if all the moments of life became a single moment—of goodbye.

Even Before I Knew

There was a dream I used to see
        even before I knew
        why this story meant so much to me.

There is a love I used to long for
        even before I knew
        why I must never have it all.

There is a sad end I used to live
        even before I knew
        this is how I was meant to begin.

Part Two

School of Lost Souls

Soul's Power: Kintsukoroi

You repair you,
> your collapsed body of clay,
> your wrecked heart of glass,
> with hopes of gold,
> confidence of diamond.

And the world shamefully witnesses—

How your soul becomes
> so beautiful
> so magical,
> just for having been
> painfully broken.

Life

This Earth is a funny planet.
      Life in it is nothing—
      but a game.

We all are players.

      Some play with toys.
      Some—
      with hearts.

Butterfly

A perfect time
       for transformation
       is when you experience
       an intense pain
       and feel simply
       out of control.

Know that
       it's time
       for the caterpillar.

To become a—
       Butterfly.

Love

One day.

One day, I told the world, that what I felt for you—was *Love*.

Today I'm not the same soul anymore. My heart isn't the same, my body isn't the same, nor are my two hands that you proudly un-held. You left me and this one lesson was instantly unlocked. I looked up above with teary eyes astoundingly wide seeing the light and glitters that hardly reveal themselves to anyone. This hurting moment of abandonment convinced me to be its student and so opening my heart, stretching my trembling hands to the unseen immensity, I've learnt—*Love* is one of the strongest weapons human beings end up using to achieve success and freedom: the two most priceless things for which hatred and wars have been destroying the world since its creation.

Being a student of ache that is universal, I learnt the rule is simple—success, through *Love,* doesn't seek anyone who is already a failure. And freedom, of course through *Love,* doesn't hunt for someone who is already a captive. Love sees no situation, no condition, no reason, no rule, no law, no right and no wrong. When it is meant to enter your life, it just enters. Yet, the success and freedom one attains through *Love,* even if this person continues to stay a failure or a captive in other matters, they would still achieve a kind of success, a kind of freedom that even the most victorious and independent people would never achieve otherwise.

However, many times we human beings end up expecting *Love* at our door when things are going wrong, too wrong, when we are half or complete failures or brutally caged or have a little bit of absolutely nothing. One midnight, all of a sudden, we just decide to stop waiting for achievements and independence to enter our lives; we just hold the hands of *Love* tightly, sometimes even grab it by the hair, and drag it along the ground toward us. We think, this, this *Love* will bring us triumph, deliver our liberty.

And thus, in our rush and anxiety and grief and fears and suffocation, to fall in *Love* we end up choosing someone who is available, reachable, who is near, and who has the ability to solve all our problems. Or maybe some. Or just one. Or who can benefit us, give us what life kept hard to reach. As a stubborn and impatient creation, amidst all our problems, we don't understand—actually we don't want to understand—that when *Love* enters you, it will continue to choose the same person for you again and again no matter what your situation and condition is. Your *Love* will choose the same person when you have everything *and* this same *Love* of yours will choose the same person even if you have nothing. Your *Love* will choose the *Love* of your life when you are a winner *and* this same *Love* of yours will continue to choose the same *Love* of your life if you are nothing but an awful failure.

In *Love*, always ask yourself these three questions: the person whom you have chosen to Love, would you choose this same person if you had *everything and if you were tremendously successful?* Ask yourself, the person whom you have chosen to *Love*, would you choose this same person if you had *a little bit in life*? Ask yourself, the person whom you have chosen to *Love*, would you choose this same person if you had *nothing and you were a complete failure with lots of restrictions and calamities*? If even a faint 'no' echoes in your heart, then your emotions and feelings and longings are not *Love*. You might have accepted that person in your life out of helplessness, or out of fear, or compulsion, insecurity, greed, selfishness, ego, pride or mistake, or even an immature decision—for any of these reasons, but not for *Love*.

When I didn't have the freedom to have *everything* I wished for, when I didn't have the option to choose what I wanted to choose, when I was nothing and I had almost something of nothing, was exactly when I wanted to have you. If ever I had just something of everything, you wouldn't have been the choice.

This is exactly what hundreds of thousands are doing right now. We pretend to be happy with whom we could. We *Love*, whom we shouldn't, whom we must not.

But whom we—could.

A Historic Lesson

Some people enter our lives
        as an answer to a hundred questions—
        that life will someday ask us
        through some destitutions.

These same people leave our lives
        as a question to a hundred answers—
        that life wouldn't give us otherwise,
        not even through any disasters.

Lack Of Love

Some people understand,
    who you are,
    reaching to the bottom of your heart,
    from a distance so far.

And surprisingly,
    some take a lifetime
    to understand who you are not,
    despite being someone so close.

Living Through Nightmares

For some,
>   they do not need
>   to fall sleep,
>   to have nightmares.

They go through them,
>   even in their waking moments,
>   feeling every fright—
>   with eyes wide open.

Know That

To be completely in love,
      with someone who loves you
      not as much,
      is what will always break you,
      in the end.

The people who mean,
      too much to you,
      will one day
      make a daily routine,
      to hurt you too much.

Ego

The greatest distance
      is not the distance
      of a thousand miles.

It is actually the distance
      we create between two souls
      whose bodies touch.

Between two souls
      who were once together,
      who were supposed to stay together.

Laughing While Bleeding

If the sun leaves at night,
        what more damage could moon do
        if it threatens the sky
        to withhold its light?

No moon, no stars,
        no new discoveries,
        can darken the universe
        more than the sun.

So when the people inside of us,
        cause our destruction,
        what more damage could be done
        by someone from the outside?

Why Do You Write?

To leave the world
        for some time,
        to rephrase myself
        and edit some parts of mine.

To put some full-stops;
        to hear, with hands,
        all that other voices
        fail to tell;

To un-live some regrets;
        un-speak some words;
        un-feel some aches,
        some mistakes.

And come back to the world
        completely different—
        absolutely ready
        to repair any of its cracks.

Poet's Poetry

Throughout history,
    poets have always been
    an unsolved mystery.

No one knows,
    if poetry is for a poet
    or a poet is for poetry.

Why they write,
    for whom they write,
    is but an unknown story.

My poems are every poet's sadness,
    through them I give the world
    a rhyme of secret victory.

Two Sides Of The Same Coin

Some truths have so much power,
      if told at the correct time,
      even the truth of extreme disloyalty
      brings oneself the title of honesty.

But the same untold truths
      will remove the veil of lies,
      showing the face of a betrayer,
      if told later by another.

Patience

By pretending,
     it didn't hurt you
     as the spine of your trust broke;

by remaining content,
     simply not knowing
     the things you wanted to know;

by continuing to smile,
     with a bullet of remorse
     lodged inside your gut;

by realising,
     every misunderstanding, every doubt,
     doesn't always need an explanation;

you do—
     the greatest justice
     to your very own self.

You Silly Girl

If his voice
>makes you forget
>you have a choice, too,

if his eyes
>make you forget
>you can see, too,

if his luring words,
>make you forget
>you can control yourself, too,

if his presence
>makes you forget,
>that you even exist,

then he is keeping you forgetful,
>preventing you from remembering,
>you are a completely different soul.

In one world,
>he would delightfully live
>two lives together.

With one life,
>he would have two bodies,
>two souls, two hearts.

But you,
>you won't be dead,
>either.

My Aim In Life

Everyday you have the choice to be whatever you want to be. If you dream of being a doctor, even before being this, you already become something: you become—its dreamer. You plan to be a destination, but even before being this, you become this—its path. You long to be someone's love and instantly you become a seeker of—love.

When they ask you what you want to be, broaden your chest, straighten up your ten legs and tell them, "When I grow up, I want to be myself." And that's it—you become you.

For whatever else you wish to be, you could only become—someone else. Or no one at all.

Remember World Remember

When a fresh new leaf splits,
>> in a season it was meant
>> to live whole,

when a new branch breaks,
>> in a phase it was supposed to
>> bear sweet berries,

when a bud withers,
>> exactly when it was
>> to bloom into a vibrant flower,

when the strongest root detaches,
>> and it can no longer
>> nourish its undeveloped parts,

remember world, remember,
>> a tree like that isn't dead;
>> it lives death by living its life.

Sometimes death isn't what happens
>> when living comes to an end;
>> sometimes death is—living, too.

Last Day Of Eternity

In love, one can always believe in loving someone until the end; but I've learnt, love isn't a belief. In love, one can always promise to always want someone no matter what happens; but I've learnt, love isn't a promise. In love, one can always challenge loving someone every single day of forever; but I've learnt, love isn't living the forever in a challenge, in words, or in confidence. In love, one can always sacrifice, one can always try, to cross the ocean, to touch the sky; but I've realised, love isn't what you did. Neither why you did. Nor how you did. Love isn't how much you used to, how much you still, or how much you will.

Love isn't what could be, what would be, what should be.

Love is standing on the last day of eternity, and saying— I've loved you, held you, every single day of forever, and *I still do*.

A Strange Punishment

They kept telling her, reminding her, warning her—*"What would people say?"* Her dreams were thrown away, her prayers left unanswered; she was told the world is bad so she must remain scared. Slowly and painfully, one day, very joyfully, she became all that people won't say—She became depressed, beautifully hopeless, and a little bit of death.

And these same people, always fearing what others would say, now call her—*a burden.*

The Ocean

It's raining incredibly. My windows keep themselves wide open with the help of the wind's strange resentment upon them. The night, sitting like a princess in the garden of stars high above, is throwing all its blackness soaked in chilly moonlight right through the windows—to me.

I swear I can clearly hear every raindrop. I can clearly hear every word that was quiet when I needed them to speak the most. I can clearly hear how every memory is still begging to finish the story of an unfinished ache. I can clearly, very clearly, hear all the parts of me, which learn no language, asking for my forgiveness for failing to brace my form and shape. At the same time, drops of pain wearing cloths made of water jump out of my eyes to sit on my lap like an innocent child.

But nothing of it kills me anymore. Nothing of it fills me with despair. Every raindrop that hits the ground so hard, breaking all of its legs, arms and all other bones, reveals to me a beautiful secret of strength, power, and transformation: that only because of falling so hard are they able to meet the stronger, the bigger part of themselves—the ocean. For the first time they witness, how this stronger and bigger part of them, this ocean, never becomes a dawn when the dawn comes and orders it to be so. It becomes the silver that shines, gold that glows. When the noon threatens, the ocean doesn't become noon. It becomes green that glitters or orange that overwhelms, or even powerfully red…and two blue radiant eyes—when the blackness hits so hard at night.

And on an inspiring sunny day of summer, the raindrop becomes so full of inspiration and courage that like a balloon filled with gas, it rises up in the sky. Even after such a hard fall, it becomes as whole as before; as fearless as it has always been. Broken legs, arms, and all other bones—all fine and set to fall back again.

When you are hurt for the first time, you become scared to be hurt again. No one bears the first taste of hurt well, believe me. When you are hurt for the second time, you suffer terribly that it happened again. The third time you are hurt, you become severely terrified that your life will be a repetition of nothing but hurt. And the repetition actually continues until the day you fall in a way that breaks your legs, arms and all the other bones of your heart. That's when you finally touch the ground. Now you are prepared to meet the ocean—the stronger, the bigger part of you—who takes the perfect form of courage and bravery and victory when different forms of ache try to scare you. Who doesn't become the ache itself. And so the hurt becomes fun, especially when you discover you don't have wings, nor are you flapping your arms, nor are you making any flying leaps…but still you are rising up. Broken legs, arms, bones—all fine and set to fall back again.

That's why we call the fall—rain.

Always washing away the dirt. And pain.

When You Find Yourself In The Wrong Place

Sometimes a place,
        a story,
        a time,
        a home,
        a world,
        doesn't need the people
        who fit in it.

Sometimes a place
        a story,
        a time,
        a home,
        a world,
        needs the people
        who don't fit in it.

That's how the rose
        beautifies, embellishes, transforms
        a whole monstrous tree,
        where only thorns should be.

Definition Of Strength

I—I am a girl: the invisible soft part of a young lady and an old woman. I may burst into tears just by seeing a withered flower in my neighbour's garden. And may continue to weep seeing a magnificent Oak tree in my backyard.

You—you don't need to hurt or break me into pieces to make me cry. I cry even when you mend my burnt hands and heal my inner wounds. I cry when I am so wonderfully whole. I cry even when you make me smile. I cry, I cry even when I am totally safe with you.

You—you don't need to give me a reason, too, to grieve. A silent word, a blank page, a beautiful empty cage, may easily make my eyes wet.

You—you don't need to give me expensive things. Just give me a teddy-bear hug. Or place me under the wide sky where I won't notice my own feet; I won't see any walls, any roofs, any barriers…and I would easily shed tears.

But don't say I cry because I am a girl, a woman and my heart is weak. Or a boy, a man, must be the reason. And never ever, tell me—never-ever—that my tears are spurious, that through them I try to trap you. Try to emotionally blackmail you. The destruction of this universe began the day it was decided to prevent boys and men from crying in order to redefine—strength. If you don't believe me, go back in history. And even the future will be clear to you.

This won't remain a world of strong bodies full of strength; this will soon become a world of extremely strong bodies, full of hardness that break exact bodies like theirs that will never get repaired.

Remember, our tears, our tears, our softness, don't make us weak. It can never be the definition of—weakness. After all, the most unbreakable hearts have been given birth by those girls and women who cry. So you and your world must decide what your own definition of strength will be: someone who is hard because of not crying, or someone who is strong because of crying.

A Forgotten Hope

I know we can go beyond the road.
    If not the real road,
    then the road of humiliation, for sure.

I know we can swim against the current.
    If not the real current,
    then the current of
    our wounded hearts, for sure.

I know we can rise up from the ocean
    after touching our fingers to its floor.
    If not the real ocean,
    then the ocean of despair, for sure.

I always knew,
    God can do beyond the things
    we think He is able to do.
    And so today I know,
    we can always go beyond the line
    we have thought we would end up on.

God gave us that power.
    God gave us that control.

What I Used To Fear Most?

That someday I would love someone; and this person would love me back, just as much. We would spend our time together, doing things that our friends would find childish. And everyone would laugh if they ever discovered our secret ways of showing love. He would know the truth but still I would lie, only to see that twinkle in his eyes. All the time he would watch me, I would pretend not to notice. Our four in the mornings would always be for God alone. Something he would share, something I would share. Sometimes he would cry, sometimes I.

Then one day everything would change. I would no longer be in his home, in his life. I wouldn't be in his photo albums, wallet or behind the colours of his office shirt. When my mug with his nickname would start to crack, he wouldn't notice. Everything that was ours in that house would now become only his. He would wake up alone, but appear... *thankful*. His autumn would be only his. So, too, its colours. And his smile would be more beautiful as he would wait for someone else to take the place that once belonged to me. Then she would start to live my mornings, and stand holding the same hands in front of the same mirror. My nights would be hers. The moon and stars outside my window, all hers, too.

In my imagination, I used to fear all these things. My mouth and lips used to go completely dry. But now we have arrived exactly at this point. And I must admit things are very different when you are actually living your fear, taking God as your only strength. God shows you how your fear comes to break you, cut you, make you bleed, so that you become stronger. And you find *no* reason why you *should stay broken.*

It makes my day, it makes me smile, to think you are doing fine in that same world, same room, same bed where once I used to be. And our memories didn't stop your time.

Nor did they stop mine.

Self Realisation

No one ruined me, actually. No one made me lonely, no one broke my heart. Every day is a different day for me not because the date is different, the month is different, the year is different; but because every day, I learn a new lesson.

So today I woke up, just like I always do. The summer sun, the dawn sky, the light breeze, the sound of the trees, everything was different. But the lesson I learnt—that was new. Today I learnt to look back and notice my own faults. Today I learnt that—that no one holds the power to ruin me, to make me lonely, to break my heart as long as I don't allow them to do so. I learnt—to understand and claim that all those days even I was wrong somewhere—is a kind of bravery that even the fearless soldiers don't show in a field of war.

Beauty Of Broken Hearts

I don't know if I'm living in the same world as yours where the day ends sharp at 12:00 p.m. and sharp at 12:01 a.m., everything restarts. Without a single stoppage, a single delay, a single pause. The murderers of hearts walk freely on the road as if nothing happened yesterday. The one who threw all my pages into the deep sea just an hour ago—sleeps so comfortably as if no injustice took place on this planet.

I can allow this brand new time to snatch the eyes away from me, the same eyes through which I have been creating an entirely different solar system. I can allow this time, that was nothing to me many years ago when I stood up on my two baby feet quicker than many, to make me shake. Today, leaving time behind, I can even disappear, easily—inside a huge plane to Palm Desert without a single complaint. I can allow time to be the road on which I run so fast that I am unable to count the cracks on the walls under my own skin.

But the twelve numbers of my clock, they shouldn't heal all my wounds. They can swirl, they can whirl and I am ready to stand right in the centre of second, minute and hour without running away or collapsing—but these three hands, they will always be too weak to catch all my pain.

Because I'm stronger right where I have been wounded.

It's Too Late

And I would change
        in a beautifully dangerous way
        that you would ache terribly to believe.

With an artist's confidence
        I would transform myself
        into an historic artwork.

You would try to understand
        the new me,
        my unbelievable recovery.

But nothing would ever be understood,
        nothing would seem real, except this—
        "It was her, it was always her."

The Healing

Suddenly in a dull afternoon,
    the rolling waves stopped coming
    back to the shore,
    simply flowing away to the unknown.

Happiness closed up its door.
    Autumn, summer, spring,
    every season left
    all the vivid colours.

Fascinating birds, too,
    stopped fluttering their feathers,
    silently sitting all day
    on the innermost branch all alone.

At last that unwanted moment
    reached its desired time;
    when the night entered the space,
    even the darkness turned away its face.

And eventually, sadness, too,
    stopped loving the sad,
    stopped loving my loneliness
    and simply left.

Freedom

My silence,
        now speaks to me
        better than ever before.

Now when I know
        I should be angry,
        I am not.

Today I turn all my wounds
        into my freedom,
        with my arms wrapped around me,
        eyes tightly closed.

Hope For The Heartbroken

In love we never
      are the losers;
      in it either we win
      or we become wiser.

Either we make someone eternal,
      Or we become—one.

The Secret To Success

Find yourself after getting lost;
    you will get the address
    of where you can
    always be found.

Love after unreciprocated love,
    you will never be wrong
    about how
    you must be loved.

Heal yourself after being wounded,
    you will become skilled at
    remaining unwounded
    despite the wounds.

Retain hope after constantly failing,
    and tell me if you haven't
    discovered for you,
    where your success is still waiting.

You are a House

There is a difference
       between a home and a house.
       A home is where you leave
       a piece of your heart.
       A piece of your soul.

A house, however, is
       where you live.

Your words, your behaviour,
       your character, your manner,
       your belief, your dreams, your wishes—
       all these together are
       the big house where you live.

It all depends on you—only you—
       how serene your home must be
       and how beautiful you want
       your house to be.

That, be it home or house,
       people come in,
       and never again want to leave.

True Success

What books failed to inspire,
    Faith was never unsuccessful.

What swords and bombs failed to accomplish,
    Faith was never unsuccessful.

What wealth and poverty failed to buy,
    Faith was never unsuccessful.

What pain failed to transform,
    Faith was never unsuccessful.

What the whole world failed to give,
    Faith was never unsuccessful.

What love failed to heal,
    Faith was never unsuccessful.

Reality Of Life

Only a few writers
        are real.

They understand
        a story with a happy ending
        is always an unfinished story.

Only a few writers know,
        the story is imperfect
        if the ending is perfect.

Only a few writers feel,
        a story shouldn't be
        like a story.

It should be
        like—Life.

Broken Hearts

Right now I am raw. My ache is raw, wound is raw. With my wet eyes squeezed and my shaky legs firmly pressed against my chest, I can taste the sharp flavour of extreme heartache in my mouth. It isn't the first time. It isn't the second time, either. It isn't even the thirty fifth time. The girl whose heart breaks even when a flower dies, how can she keep track of such huge numbers?

All I remember is pain. Unbearable pain.

And I am crying now. Hard. But I am still brave enough to tell you—this: We are not defined by what happened to us. We are what God believed us to be before blessing us with this extreme heartache. Not everyone was, or is, or will be chosen to endure this trial that is powerful enough to shatter human hearts. The sun may break and never be fixed. The sky may crumble down and never be restored. The earth may crack everywhere and cause devastation to the entire universe but believe me, if a human heart breaks, crumbles or cracks, it means this heart is powerful. It means the owner of this heart knows the incredible art to repair souls, to stitch souls, to make souls simply incredible.

Not everyone can own a broken heart. Not even if they want to. Believe me. One has to be incredibly strong to own a shattered heart.

But in case you are wondering why you have been

chosen to be so powerful, then know that someone once said, "Great design is achieved not when there is nothing left to add, but when there is nothing left to take away." The process of breaking hearts is only to show you the pieces that are preventing you from being a great design, a design that is really incredible. Or you may say a design that is unbelievable. So that you can remove those unnecessary pieces of you and be what you should be: as powerful as your heartache.

Have patience, have faith in God's decision to choose you for this break, for this grief—and like me—even when completely broken and unaware of how things would become better and when time would heal me—believe that the worst sadness releases the best happiness. And time? Time isn't meant to heal you; the hurting itself is healing you. Now. And one day, when you are not ready at all, when you aren't wearing your best clothes, when you aren't looking your best and haven't sprayed yourself with your favourite perfume, when you are fighting sleep, staring at a queue of ants on your ceiling, you will be informed—

Congratulations! Your broken heart has been successfully transformed into the best incredible design. Are you ready to conquer the world?

In This World

Some dreams,
      aren't meant
      to be seen.

Some things,
      aren't meant
      to be desired.

Some longings,
      some wishes, some unrealities,
      shouldn't be hoped for.

Some prayers,
      should always be there,
      unanswered.

So that you understand
      this isn't
      the real world.

      It is some other.

Trust In God

What you love,
 what you desire,
 what you seek,

Defines who you are.

You love it,
 you desire it,
 you seek it,
 because it loves you,
 it desires you,
 it seeks you.

They were all meant for you.

Maybe you got it yesterday;
 if not, maybe today;
 if not, maybe you'll get it
 tomorrow.

In the end—
 you will get it all for sure;
 in the same form,
 in the same size,
 in the same amount.

The End

They wrongly claim,
        that a story is incomplete
        as long as
        there is an unhappy ending.
I say,
        as long as there is no happy beginning,
        not a single story
        ever approaches a sad ending.

Part Three

Darling It's Me: Love!

Soul's Light

It took all the darkness
       of the universe
       to darken me deep inside,
       so that I could see you,

I could know—
       who you are.

After all, the brightest of stars
       is only meant to be discovered
       in the darkest of nights.

A Dedication

He is the gorgeous hero
        of every romantic novel
        she rereads.

She isn't,
        his beautiful heroine—
        merely a dedicated reader
        more promising to him.

A Powerful Revenge

I don't believe in loathing. I don't think of revenge. I don't curse, I don't forever suffer. Nothing angers me, at least not for too long.

And at least, not anymore.

But today let me tell you one of the greatest secrets. The greatest kind of relief comes from forgiveness. It sets you free. So forgive. But remember, sometimes the greatest kind of punishment is—forgiveness, too. Sometimes those whom we forgive, forgiveness become their greatest punishment.

A Celebration

Of failure and flaws,
        that awaken the soul.

Of love that tears apart,
        to give birth to a phenomenon.

Of all the impossible accomplishments,
        through hope and endurance.

The Happy Beginning

This God's universe, is being rebuilt by broken hearts with unfulfilled wishes and an ache that hurts. Tortured girls, end up winning the Noble peace prize. Boys with no hands, teach confidence and success to all those with beautiful hands. Childless women, become well-known as the mothers of thousands. Men whose wives died suddenly, work day and night, representing love and light.

The sadness of strange souls, is constantly producing happy beginnings. And so to the world who once told me *"You will never heal,"* I just want to say—today someone said to me, *"Hey, you healed me."*

Beauty Of Love

Somewhere far,
        there is a hidden library
        with golden books that are
        miraculously everlasting.

All the souls,
        who have the secret sorrow,
        caress the books' typewriter font,
        and live all the lives they wish for.

The owner
        is a mysterious man,
        elusive of our
        searching glances.

Some say he isn't a writer;
        neither a rhymester, they say;
        however, only he has a heart
        of words—eternally undiscovered,

with enough power
        to transform me
        into forever,
        into an entire breathing universe.

The Beginning

You were right there before my eyes, unfolding little by little all the surprises life could ever offer. I could clearly see what my ears were hearing and hear exactly what my eyes were seeing. It still tires me to realise how a human being as ordinary as everyone else could be so visible and audible just by living. And so for the first time, in a very long time—I instantly understood what I was meant to understand in this small world.

I witnessed every season this world has to offer me long before meeting you. I know exactly how a burning sun behind melting clouds looks and how ancient stars look in the palms of a night river. I perfectly memorised the lyrics of the songs morning birds sing, and what the evening breeze murmurs to midnight. I have seen how a thousand pieces of the one sky swim and how the calmness and serenity of oceans fly. I have even finished meeting people who could break me, who could have built me, fixed me beautifully. But with you, I don't want to go back to witness, to experience, to feel life's infinite beauties once again. Because in what went on before, what happened before, there was never the beginning that I have to go back. There were only endings. And whatever there is that has an end, an ending, can have a beginning but it can never be—*the* beginning.

It is, *the* beginning, right from you—from here, from today, from this very moment, this nothing or everything—

that I want to witness each and everything, I want to experience life and see how many millions and millions of mysteries life has the strength to unfold in front of me, I want to feel life, I want to taste it, tease it, make it laugh. I so madly want to be carried away to anywhere you are found, to anywhere you want to be found. I want to see, feel, and witness it all not again but for the first ever beginning of our eternity.

In uncountable moments that I lived before yet never was I born, in uncountable footsteps that I left behind yet never had I existed there, you are the best thing that ever happened to me…ever happening to me.

You are the best thing I began.

Season Of Falling

The morning is beating outside as only my heart is meant to beat inside. With feelings squeezing out autumn's colours, with yellow sunshine tying long flared skirts of blue around hidden wind's waist in the far horizon, my life has started to change bit by bit, little by little.

From thoughts of you to thoughts about you, the ink of longing flows through me the way childhood of rivers flow through mountains and hills. Falling into you, the way a star falls through the infinite miracles of the universe, how difficult it is to live in such a small body with weight, with only two hands, only two legs yet not a single wing to fly away.

How breathtaking, to see dreams dreaming me; and to wander full of wonders—holding my hands, where this love is taking me.

First Love

The world would teach you,
　　　the first love
　　　is the hardest
　　　to get over.

You can't love anyone
　　　that intensely
　　　more than once,
　　　in a lifetime.

Yet the moment,
　　　this one last person
　　　takes a determined step
　　　in your direction,

all others—
　　　become a mistake.
　　　A forgettable regret.
　　　A lesson so priceless.

....

How should he be?

He should be someone who holds your hand and hears your
heart. Because this. This is love.

Butterflies In The Stomach

When you repeat everything that is old between us, that already happened once, or a thousand times—an affectionate call, a tease full of hopes, a push to never give up, a consolation, a deep concern, a thank-you hug, a cute apology holding the ears, a night—it seems and sounds so fresh, new and gorgeous. Every time you tell me something romantic, in the blink of an eye it becomes untold. Tell this to me again and I would fall in your arms just the way I did when I heard it for the first time.

Every wonderful feeling you express, in a second becomes unexpressed. Say it again and you would again witness there's nothing in the universe that can't be fixed. What was believable becomes unbelievable: that cheerfulness, that togetherness, that madness. Even every touch of yours, so quickly, becomes absolutely untouched. As if we've come to know each other just now. As if we are going to fall in love only now. As if every best thing that took place between us before, is taking place again now.

But for the very first time.

When Love Surrenders

There is a melancholy
    I treasure,
    it is sweeter to me
    than any other pleasure.

There is a tight grip
    that explodes flowers from the ground,
    perfuming my heart
    in celebration of being found.

A stare,
    that drags my complete self,
    if I could give more than that,
    I would.

He And I

He and I
  entrust each other,
  fearlessly, courageously—
  with the most fragile part of us.

This delicate part keeps us stronger
  than the hurricane
  as long as it stays—
  firmly unbroken.

It is also of the nature
  to destroy its owner completely
  to sharp pieces of broken mirror,
  once either of us breaks it even a little.

Crumbling our hearts,
  this part's brokenness
  would throw us away,
  anytime, anywhere, wherever.

Yet he gives away
  his world to protect it.
  I, too—
  happily sacrifice mine.

An Old Friend

To know you,
>> is to be knowing
>> the nameless soul
>> my body has been owning.

The more
>> you unfold yourself,
>> the more
>> I am unfolded.

As if
>> you are a mirror;
>> I am the reflection
>> breathing there.

What I Love About You

That the things that once were,
  so perfect without you—
  the words of a novel,
  the sunset horizon,
  the singing ocean,
  the summer butterflies,

one day started to appear,
  so very incomplete,
  so very imperfect
  and empty,
  just without you.

Until

The world was invisible,
        inaudible and disconnected.

Until you were the one
        with whom I shared my presence.

Until, to hear my silence,
        you made all the attempts.

Until all your dreams
        found a home in my name.

He

His friends,
> ring me up,
> when he doesn't
> give them time enough.

His mother,
> asks me first,
> if he ever,
> feels hurt.

When I walk
> into a gathering he is enjoying,
> everyone notices,
> he is awfully stammering.

Her Effects

When I'm
        with her,
        I split into
        two halves.

Half of me shakes,
        my knees go weak,
        my heart entirely forgets
        how and where to beat.

Half of me grows serene,
        full of strength;
        no matter what ails me,
        I can face all the battles.

An Adventure

The more
       you urge,
       the less
       I prevent.

The stronger
       your hope,
       the weaker
       my despair.

My Name

And if only
> you could see,
> how those small universes
> in every part of my body,
> light up a thousand lanterns
> as you repeat
> my name,
> my name,
> my name.

Sometimes in a way
> that entertains you,
> entices you,
> fulfills you;
> sometimes,
> you say,
> it's an alluring poetry,
> whose every verse
> can rewrite
> your entire history.

....

"But I'm so imperfect for you," she says, still weeping. He presses his forehead into her temple and closes his eyes. After a few minutes he replies, "Yes, so very perfectly imperfect."

Sorry

To the mustn'ts,
        to the shouldn'ts.
        the don'ts,
        the won'ts,
        the impossibles,
        the nevers,
I couldn't give him—
        a no.

Not for once.

You

Where there is love,
       I always fall for you.
       Where there is time,
       I find you.
       Where there is sound,
       I hear…

       your voice.

The sea was just a sea;
       but you became its green deepness.
       The sky was just a sky;
       now you are its blue vastness.
       The rose was a red rose;
       now you are…

       it's melting fragrance.

If the beauty of you
       is one wing
       of summer butterflies,
       the other one—is my existence.
       My state of being able to be seen.

I wish to keep flying
       in the colourful garden of forever.

Tu Me Manques

The distance slithering,
      from me to you,
      is a trace of my inner blue.

The moon you see,
      always wets its light
      perching on my longing eyes.

My lashes squeeze
      a pair of dark aches,
      when the midnight whispers.

It's not that I only miss you extremely,
      it's that—
      you are missing from me.

Pinch Me

To tell
> how I felt the unfelt.
> To touch
> what seems unbelievable.
> To show
> what I don't know.
> To repeat
> all that they never teach.
> To be born
> after living a long life.
> To love
> after hating the whole world.
> To laugh,
> to laugh
> to laugh madly,
> I don't know
> if life is happening—
> like a dream.
> Or in a dream.
> Or if even—
> this is life.

Madly In Love

In the mystique of our togetherness,
      all my longings have been beautified.

Green darkness constantly twinkling
      to make love to all my blue lights.

My body became a secret forest,
      here only fairies enter to hide.

Helplessness

To know,
        your deepest love
        was once in so much grief,
        and because of it, still is,
        and would be,

adds an unseen torture
        to the grief you were,
        and still are,
        and would always be.

My Empty Body
(The First Type Of Loneliness)

Can you see
     this ground, this sky, this me?

All of these beautifully disappear
     when you are with me right here.

You own my heart,
     you will always own my heart;
     only you are its beautiful art.

But when you disappear,
     even if I'm the focus of the crowd,
     I look for myself,
     here and there.

I look everywhere.

But find myself
     nowhere,
     not anywhere.

Interchange Of Souls

The way you want me,
      the way I want you,
         it's like a direct interchange of souls
         took place long ago between us.

The humorous whispers you repeat,
      from me the smiles you receive,
         is and always will be—
         our most favourite exchange.

His Proposal

"Come into my heart?" He proposes to her, dropping himself on his left knee after the horrible argument.

"And why should I?" She demands and returns to him the comb which is fulfilling the job of a rose.

"Because you...you are complicated." He quickly and very tightly clasps her hands between his own before she beats his unbreakable chest.

"Yes, you are," he heartlessly confirms, "You are the only one for whom two vast wings, larger than the world, stronger than my backbone, grow out of my back." Her hands fighting against his suddenly become calm. "Don't worry, I won't be able to fly away," his breaths carefully perched, one after another, on her shoulders as he pulls her close. "These wings are complicated. They fly not when I keep you, but when you keep yourself—in me."

Magical Hug

It's so tight
     and so hard.

It's so very tender.

That by the time you release,
     all my broken pieces get fixed.

And I recover.

Perfect Unsatisfaction

To have you,
> you and only you—in my life,
> is an amazingly satisfying unsatisfaction.

You are the only one
> who, always and always,
> keeps me magically satisfied
> in a way as if—

I was never before satisfied,
> no matter how many times
> you have already
> given yourself—to me.

As if I don't want to be satisfied,
> no matter how perfectly
> you have already,
> satisfied me.

As if I can never be satisfied,
> no matter how dangerously
> you love me,
> and pour yourself—into me.

Language of Love

I tried to write you down. The way your smile tickles the very inner skin of my heart. The way your white and yellow butterfly-words follow me everywhere. The way, your honey-melting stare hugs the depth of my wandering eyes.

But I failed.

I don't know if I should be angry with the chaste black ink of my pen, or with the whiteness of my diary's page. I changed the colour of my ink again and again. I wrote in blue, in yellow, in red. I crumpled up the pages one after another and turned the house into a perfect mess. Or was it me who doesn't know this unwritten language too well? You laughed crazily that night when I asked, *I think I should learn a few more languages to express you; should I go for Arabic, French and Spanish first?*

It truly saddened me a bit.

Love has one language, you whispered clutching me from behind with your whole body. *It can never be written in letters and books, or ever be conveyed in songs and soundless sounds. It is only expressed by how you make someone feel—your hands discovering new worlds in a tight hug, in a firm grip; your fulfilled-promises painting the whole solar system right on your beloved's backbone, keeping it forever unbreakable; your two eyes doing what only a thousand hands of yours were supposed to do; and your continuous magical whisperings—This. This. This.*

My beloved, all else is a body without five senses.

Jealousy

The world never understood—a girl.

When she finally accepts his proposal, no matter how temptingly he speaks about another woman, or how jolly he becomes with a different woman, her jealousy isn't for this—other woman.

Or if the story is like this, that she chooses him to love, but he chooses some other woman to love instead of her, her jealousy isn't for this—other woman.

Or even if he betrays her, cheats on her, or lies to her because of another woman, a girl's jealousy is never for this—other woman.

It is always for those women, with enticing eyes and immense glows, who want him so badly, it is always for those girls who seem so perfect, who are so lucky by fate, yet he ignores them all—focusing all his attention only to her soul.

First Fight

The first fight,
      is so very hurtful,
      yet impossibly—
      romantic and wonderful.

They disagree,
      and all of a sudden,
      love becomes
      a catastrophe.

She cries
      and temptingly threatens him,
      he pretends to fear
      and constantly apologises.

Gradually, very softly, they fall hard
      into each other's arms,
      for a moment that takes—
      a few weeks to pass.

Art Of Compromise

If things don't work,
        the way I want, the way you want;
        if things do not go right
        between the two of us;

if something I do,
        hurts you;
        if something you say,
        blooms dark night in my day;

if something one of us likes,
        the other dislikes;
        if you are yellow and I'm white;
        if yours is North and South is mine;

if my past is good,
        and yours is bad;
        if everything seems hard,
        and a few things come easy;

still amidst all our wounds, in all our moments,
        in all our stories and fables,
        during our lives, even after deaths,
        we will only remain ours truly.

You will ask, I will answer;
   you will answer, I will ask;
   being two different bodies,
   we will possess the same soul-love.

.

Our Discussion

I can give you a thousand reasons to make you stay. I can give you a lot of new beginnings to all your bad endings of yesterdays. In all your sad winters, I can gift you the hopes of summer. What makes you content can always be my heart's colour.

However, throughout my childhood I saw how one doll was never enough to arrange a wedding ceremony. If I ever noticed there was no star near the half-moon, I kept waiting all night for a star to twinkle somewhere near. When the flowers of my small garden showed me a different beauty of theirs being withered, I sprayed all over them my favourite perfume's whisper. And while reading love stories, I still keep searching for that one page, for that one sentence, where the two fall for each other.

Hard.

Whatever I can do for you, I can do it beyond the boundary of all my limits. Whatever something I can give you, it can always be my—everything. Anything. The whole thing. However my thousand reasons to make you stay, my new beginnings to all your bad endings, my hopes of summer in all your sad winters, my heart with the colour of your contentment—all are hopeless—without you as the other doll; without you as the twinkling star; without you as the fragrance; without you as one of the two.

If you don't make an effort, too, to solve these arguments, to heal these hurts, to keep each other closer than our jugular veins, the thing is, even the whole universe won't be able to prevent the final goodbye.

....

You understand me, right? she questions.
I understand not a single thing else, he confirms.

Impossible Adverb

"How many days are there in forever?" he inquired.

"I can't be counted," Forever replied with extreme pride.

Sadness becomes his tone. "But I want to know the number of those uncountable days!"

"And what are you going to do with that?" Forever shot him an irritated glance.

"I need another perfect word, another more forever word; you seem too short and meaningless, and unfair, when I…I look into her eyes," he replied, eyes wide.

Forever shook his head and slapped his forehead in disbelief.

Answer Me

And you love me more, you say?
> That all of me leaking out
> from all of your cells of hope,
> didn't happen in just one day.

How can I show you,
> how you pierce yourself
> into my skin, my bones, my soul,
> repairing all my bruises, my lacerations?

How fiercely
> you rip my heart wide open;
> how gently
> you sweep out all its sorrow?

A Promise

One doesn't
      need to be one
      so that the person they love—
      forever stays as the only one.

My life is one, but it need not be.
      My heart is one, but it need not be.
      Neither the soul needs to be one
      nor my body.

In a hundred lifetimes, with a million bodies,
      a thousand hearts, a million souls,
      you would always be, wholly,
      my one and only.

Pens Of A Poet

When I go out shopping, every single thing I like, I instantly buy for myself. When I see a mysterious diary, it reminds me of a close friend who binds all her sorrows and tears within pages that can never speak. She isn't a sad girl. It is just that through sadness—she heals her own sadness. So I buy this diary for me. Last time when I noticed a white wallet in a corner of a gift gallery silently waiting for me to notice it, I knew exactly who deserves to carry it. After all, I saw his wife's favourite earring in his wallet. His gorgeous wife still believes she lost it on her brother's wedding day. So I buy this wallet for me.

Every greeting card with a big red heart, and fancy font, can never make me think of anybody other than my beloved mother. Mothers can't be expressed. They must not be. Sometimes beautifully crafted words, can partially express the feelings. So I buy the card for me. And amazingly, I know exactly the person who knocks on my heart's door when I touch the dry paint of a mystifying dark painting with my five fingers, smell a withered flower still powerfully attached to its lively stem, or taste a melted ice cream. So I buy them all. Just for me.

And when I return home, I feel like the owner of a secret treasure. I believe that at that moment nobody is wealthier than me. These are the things I like to buy for myself. And use as excuses and opportunities to give a piece of myself to the people who matter most to me. Through gifts I give myself. I gift myself. And if someone forgets me, or ever wants to, if someone stops from letting me know where life has taken them or if it's still a sad winter when they wake up on bright summer days, I offer their pieces, their shares, to the world—through my pen.

If you are wondering what object reminds me of you and I'm compelled to buy it for myself, my answer will always be—*pens*.

Ameen

On every page that I am written,
     in every place that I am a story,
     in every moment that I am in me,
     may you get written as mine only.

When tears leave you unanswered,
     heartache makes you beg for sleep,
     may my happiness, my laughter,
     be the ground to firm your feet.

As much as I desire you,
     may I receive you just as much;
     that you, me, every part of ours,
     live for each other, in each other.

A Fairy Tale

Once in a while,
     life opens up for us,
     a gate guarded by dragons
     of—*once upon a time* kingdoms.

He turns
     into the— *charming prince,*
     I discover myself as—
     the beautiful princess.

With an indestructible hope and some confidence,
     we beat the dragons together,
     conquer the vast palace
     of our very own—*fairytale forever.*

In love, *endings* must not exist
     even if in it
     we are meant to be *happy.*

Instead of the last page
     of—*and they lived happily ever after,*
     we become each others'—
     the next chapter.

A Thousand You

On one hand, we meet a lot of people in our lives. On the other hand, for so many different reasons many of them become the souls we tremendously love.

When my five year old neighbour told me her favourite colour is sky blue, I was so excited and told her that it's your favourite, too. She blushed dramatically. I teased her asking if she would like to be your second love, to which she instantly said no as you are much taller than she and she couldn't consider always standing on her toes. She, however, gifted me her sky blue frock and I promised I would keep it. Forever.

Two of my cousins have eyes exactly like yours: black yet breathtakingly glowing. They rapidly blink of pride every time I remind them and together we laugh so much.

Even the way you wrinkle your forehead when you are trying to act dead handsome in front of me, is the same way my new classmate does when she is confused. I become breathless and tell her to be fearless when she asks for help with class notes. And the newborn baby we went to see a few days back, do you remember I was laughing so hard? Because that baby sleeps exactly like you; his mouth wide open. I told my aunt the baby's name must be as yours and the baby is mine, too, from now on. She agreed but promised to tease me for the rest of my life. I hate you for that.

Okay, I don't.

I can't.

Last month I met Edward Cullen and Bella Swan in a library between two crispy pages. I made high jumps from page to page, from one mind-blowing word to another, from one wondrous scene to another, and kept looking at him full of wonder. His rhythm of love was almost like yours, believe me— "And so the lion fell in love with the lamb…" Edward murmured in a paragraph that holds the whole twilight world. Bella looked away, hiding her eyes, thrilled at the words.

"What a stupid lamb," Bella sighed.

"What a sick, masochistic lion."

But as Bella might freak out seeing me admiring Edward so much, I came out of their world as quickly as possible. How badly I wish she knew you. How badly I wish someday she meets us two, too, in a library between two crispy pages.

There has always been a part of you in people I meet or pass by or read. If not their height, then your style. If not their face, then at least the way you smile. I start to love all these people more than you. Because when I'm with you, I'm with the love of my life. But when I'm with them, I carefully notice something of you through them, and I fall in love with you. Again.

I am sure, amidst the huge crowd of my town, if you someday shout your own name out loud, a lot of people will definitely stop and approach you saying they know this name, this you—because you have their t-shirts; some will say your perfume matches theirs; some like the coffee of the café you visit on weekends; some sell your favourite chocolate coffee; and some have the ancient poetry you have been searching for so long.

Everybody has something of you, like you. But nobody is you. Not even near to. Yet if I ever lose you, know that I would carry a pain that weighs of losing a whole town full of souls I tremendously love. I would lose a thousand of you. Perhaps a million. It isn't that no one would find me after the town's destruction. It is that I would never find anyone ever again.

Not even myself.

A Thank You Note

When they broke my trust
        before even building it,
        you fulfilled a trust
        even before you owned it.

You heard my silence
        when I couldn't hear or speak;
        wounded by their invisible hands,
        with your visible heart,
        you have healed me.

Sweet Dreams

My eyes get closed,
        and it's you,
        it's always been you,
        a hundred skies, a thousand moons.

And a hope.

That I am there in your thoughts, too,
        to keep you up all night
        and when I fall asleep,
        it's your eyes that get closed.

Index

Part I

Soul's Void   3
The Change   4
Inequality   5
An Unfair Loss   6
Complicated We   7
Unpromising   8
Blank History   9
When You Hurt   10
The Saddest Thing   11
Crying In The Shower   12
False Empathy   13
Mean   14
Self Torture   15
The Unexpressed Ache   16
Heartbreaker   17
One Way Love   18
A Black Lie   19
Misunderstanding   20
It's Over   21
Closure   22
When There's Nothing Left
To Say   23
Moving On   24
Broken Dreams   25
Loving Him   26
When We Two Parted   27
I Am Nowhere   28
I Don't Want To Know   29

Well Wishes   30
How?   31
A Rootless Wanderer   32
Hope That Only Hurts   33
Happiness   34
Generous Grief   35
The Universe
Through My Window
(The Second Type Of
Loneliness)   36
A Meaningless Expectation
38
A Prayer That Came True
39
Stranger   40
My Wasted Sacrifice   41
Emptiness   42
Sshhhh!   43
Remembering You In
My Forgetfulness   44
Treacherous Market Of Love
45
Winter Cries   46
A Melancholy Soul   47
Black Sun   48
Shackles Of Iron   49
Disappearance Of Time   50
Malaise   51
Sadly Ever After   52
Sad Girls   54

Secret Sorrows   55
Strange You   56
Unexpressed Feelings   57
Flashbacks   58
Her Nights   59
Special Power (Part One)
60
Special Power (Part Two)   62
I Wonder   64
Thunderstorm   65
If   66
The Difference   67
Law Of Conversion   68
A Lovesickness   70
Never Again   71
When Hands Unhold   72
A Cruel Reminder   73
Poet's Last Line   74
Illogical Truth   75
A Question   76
The Heartless Girl   77
Unreachable Soul   80
Release   81
Life Goes On (Part One)   82
Life Goes On (Part Two)   84
Even Before I Knew   85

Part II

Soul's Power: Kintsukoroi
89
Life   90
Butterfly   91
Love   92
A Historic Lesson   95
Lack Of Love   96
Living Through Nightmares
97
Know That   98
Ego   99
Laughing While Bleeding
100
Why Do You Write?   101
Poet's Poetry   102
Two Sides Of The Same Coin
103
Patience   104
You Silly Girl   105
My Aim In Life   106
Remember World Remember
107
Last Day Of Eternity   108
A Strange Punishment   109
The Ocean   110
When You Find Yourself In
The Wrong Place   112
Definition Of Strength   113
A Forgotten Hope   115
What I Used To Fear Most?
116
Self Realisation   118
Beauty Of Broken Hearts
119
It's Too Late   120
The Healing   121
Freedom   122
Hope For The Heartbroken
123
The Secret To Success   124
Home   125
True Success   126
Reality Of Life   127

Broken Hearts   128
In This World   130
Trust In God   131
The End   132

Part III

Soul's Light   135
A Dedication   136
A Powerful Revenge   137
A Celebration   138
The Happy Beginning   139
Beauty Of Love   140
The Beginning   141
Season Of Falling   143
First Love   144
Butterflies In The Stomach
145
When Love Surrenders   146
He And I   147
An Old Friend   148
What I Love About You
149
Until   150
He   151
Her Effects   152
An Adventure   153
My Name   154
Sorry   155
You   156
Tu Me Manques   157
Pinch Me   158
Madly In Love   159
Helplessness   160
My Empty Body

(The First Type Of
Loneliness)   161
Interchange Of Souls   162
His Proposal   163
Magical Hug   164
Perfect Unsatisfaction   165
Language Of Love   166
Jealousy   168
First Fight   169
Art Of Compromise   170
Our Discussion   172
Impossible Adverb   174
Answer Me   175
A Promise   176
Pens Of A Poet   177
Ameen   179
A Fairy Tale   180
A Thousand You   181
A Thank You Note   184
Sweet Dreams   185

21066175R00121

Printed in Great Britain
by Amazon